PENGUIN EDITION

PRENTICE HALL
LITERATURE

Step ... EP+
Rea... ...ok

Indiana

PEARSON
Prentice Hall

Boston, Massachusetts
Upper Saddle River, New Jersey

Copyright © by Pearson Education, Inc., publishing as Pearson Prentice Hall, Upper Saddle River, New Jersey 07458. All rights reserved. Printed in the United States of America. This publication is protected by copyright, and permission should be obtained from the publisher prior to any prohibited reproduction, storage in a retrieval system, or transmission in any form or by any means, electronic, mechanical, photocopying, recording, or likewise. The publisher hereby grants permission to reproduce these pages, in part or in whole, for classroom use only, the number not to exceed the number of students in each class. Notice of copyright must appear on all copies. For information regarding permission(s), write to Rights and Permissions Department.

Pearson Prentice Hall™ is a trademark of Pearson Education, Inc.
Pearson® is a registered trademark of Pearson plc.
Prentice Hall® is a registered trademark of Pearson Education, Inc.

ISBN 0-13-361731-9

1 2 3 4 5 6 7 8 9 10   10 09 08 07 06

Table of Contents

About the
Step Up to the ISTEP+ Reading Workbook

The *Step Up to the ISTEP+ Reading Workbook* is designed to provide students with practice and preparation for the **Indiana Statewide Testing for Educational Progress–Plus** (ISTEP+) for English Language Arts. The state of Indiana requires all of its students to take this exam in grades 3 through 8 and 10.

With the strong foundational skills that practice with this test aims to refine, students can expect to apply their knowledge in testing situations, in their daily schoolwork, and in real life.

The *Step Up to the ISTEP+ Reading Workbook* contains two parts:

Part 1 includes three weeks of ISTEP+ skills practice leading up to test day.

☐ **Week 1** includes guided practice with the twelve individual reading skills addressed on the ISTEP+. Week 1 ends with a short, untimed ISTEP+ Practice Test.

☐ **Week 2** provides practice with each of the three main groups of reading skills assessed on the ISTEP+. These include Reading Comprehension; Literary Analysis; and Word Recognition, Fluency and Vocabulary Development. Practice with these skills is followed by a longer ISTEP+ Practice Test that also includes an independent writing prompt just like the one on the ISTEP+ Writing Assessment.

☐ **Week 3** allows students to apply all of the skills, tips, and knowledge that they learned in Weeks 1 and 2 by taking three full-length practice tests that look exactly like the ISTEP+. These will provide students with the opportunity to see all of their reading and language skills in action and to be well prepared on test day.

Part 2 includes weekly worksheets that provide practice with skills covered in the *Prentice Hall Literature* **textbook.**

Features of this practice include the following:

- ☐ Skills review written in ISTEP+ multiple-choice question format
- ☐ Ongoing practice with ISTEP+ open-ended questions
- ☐ Monthly practice with ISTEP+ style independent writing prompts

In addition, all items in Part 1 of the *Step Up to ISTEP+ Reading Workbook* are correlated to an individual Academic Standard. This will help students refine specific skills that they may not have mastered. Correlations to the ISTEP+ Practice Tests are included in both the student workbook and this Answer Key. Because not all the Academic Standards lend themselves to a pencil and paper test, we have only listed the Standards that correspond to test questions. You can find full length Standards listings in both the *Indiana Prentice Hall Literature: The Penguin Edition* student and teacher editions.

Lastly, use the Editing Checklist and ISTEP+ Scoring Rubrics to check students' writing and assess their responses to the open-ended questions Writing Assessment sample prompts.

Introduction to the ISTEP+

Each year, Indiana students in grades 3 through 8 and 10 are required to participate in the **Indiana Statewide Testing for Educational Progress-Plus (ISTEP+).** This test includes two sections: a Basic and an Applied Skills section. The Basic Skills section contains multiple-choice questions, while the applied skills section contains multiple-choice and open-ended questions as well as a writing prompt. In both cases, the multiple-choice questions are machine scored, while the open-ended questions and the writing prompt are hand scored.

Introduction to the ISTEP+ Writing Assessment

The ability to communicate clearly and effectively in writing is critical in this day and age. This is why educators in Indiana require students to participate in the ISTEP+ Writing Assessment, which requires students to organize their thoughts and express them clearly, logically, and legibly.

In order to prepare your students for the Writing Assessment, reinforce the steps in the writing process when providing practice with ISTEP+ style writing prompts. The *Step Up to ISTEP+ Reading Workbook* provides six Writing Assessment sample prompts. In addition, you can use the "Tackling Questions on the ISTEP+" feature in the student workbook to review strategies for taking the Writing Assessment.

This includes:

Determining purpose: Teach students to read the prompt slowly in order to determine the purpose of what they are required to write.

Pre-writing and drafting: Work with students to plan their writing. Familiarize students with different strategies to brainstorm, organize, and draft their ideas. This step will not be scored on the ISTEP+, but they will be provided with space to complete it.

Revision: Once students have developed the basic framework for their piece, they should focus on the content, organization, and overall message of their writing.

Editing: Students should check their writing for paragraph structure, grammar, spelling, punctuation, and capitalization. The Editing Checklist reminds students to complete this step.

Completion of draft: Once students have completed the above steps in the writing process, it is complete. This is the only version that will be scored against the 6-point Writing Applications Rubric and the 4-point Language Conventions Rubric. Drafts will be scored with the understanding that student writing is a first draft. These rubrics can be found on page xi of the *Step Up to ISTEP+ Reading Workbook* and on page viii of this Answer Key.

Introduction to Reading/Writing Tasks

Part 2 of the ISTEP+ is what Indiana refers to as the Applied Skills section. This section includes a reading/writing task that requires students to demonstrate their reading comprehension of a narrative or informational selection. This includes one or two passages, along with related multiple-choice questions, open-ended questions, and one extended-response question. All student responses should be garnered from the text. All questions in Parts 1 and 2 of the *Step Up to ISTEP+ Reading Workbook* are written in the ISTEP+ style. In addition, the workbook contains five ISTEP+ Practice Tests.

While multiple-choice questions are scored by machine, rubrics are used to score the open-ended questions. These rubrics were developed to ensure that students' responses are scored objectively. All of these rubrics are included in both the *Step Up to ISTEP+ Reading Workbook* as well as this Answer Key. Make it an ongoing practice to review student work against their criteria.

The three different rubric types include the following:

Language Conventions

The extended-response question is scored against this rubric, which evaluates how well students use conventions such as paragraphing, grammar, word usage, and spelling. This rubric also assesses the independent writing prompt.

Extended-Response Writing Applications Overview

The extended-response question is also scored against the Extended-Response Writing Applications Overview that assesses how well students organize and communicate their thoughts.

Reading Comprehension

This 2-point rubric is used to score open-ended questions. If a student provides a response that is not listed, but that is supported by the selection, the student should receive credit.

All ISTEP+ rubrics are included on pages xi–xiv in the *Step Up to ISTEP+ Reading Workbook* and on pages viii–xi in this Answer Key.

ISTEP+ Scoring Rubrics

The following rubrics are used to score writing on the ISTEP+. Scores reflect the range of excellence in written responses to the assignment. The broad categories define the score ranges for the writing assignment and for the range of skills among students.

ISTEP+ Writing Applications Rubric

This rubric is used to score responses to the Writing Assessment prompts.

Score Level	Ideas and Content Does the writing sample:	Organization Does the writing sample:	Style Does the writing sample:	Voice Does the writing sample:
6	☐ Fully accomplish the task? ☐ Include thorough, relevant, and complete ideas?	☐ Organize ideas logically?	☐ Exhibit exceptional word usage? ☐ Demonstrate exceptional writing technique?	☐ Demonstrate effective adjustment of language and tone to task and reader?
5	☐ Fully accomplish the task? ☐ Include many relevant ideas?	☐ Organize ideas logically?	☐ Exhibit very good word usage? ☐ Demonstrate very good writing technique?	☐ Demonstrate effective adjustment of language and tone to task and reader?
4	☐ Accomplish the task? ☐ Include relevant details?	☐ Organize ideas logically?	☐ Exhibit good word usage? ☐ Demonstrate good writing technique?	☐ Demonstrate an attempt to adjust language and tone to task and reader?
3	☐ Minimally accomplish the task? ☐ Include some relevant details?	☐ Exhibit an attempt to organize ideas logically?	☐ Exhibit ordinary word usage? ☐ Demonstrate average writing technique?	☐ Demonstrate an attempt to adjust language and tone to task and reader?
2	☐ Only partially accomplish the task? ☐ Include few relevant details?	☐ Exhibit a minimal attempt to organize ideas logically?	☐ Exhibit minimal word usage? ☐ Demonstrate minimal writing technique?	☐ Demonstrate language and tone that may be inappropriate to task and reader?
1	☐ Fail to accomplish the task? ☐ Include very few relevant ideas?	☐ Organize ideas illogically?	☐ Exhibit less than minimal word usage? ☐ Demonstrate less than minimal writing technique?	☐ Demonstrate language and tone that may be inappropriate to task and reader?

ISTEP+ Language Conventions Rubric

This rubric applies to both writing assessment and extended-responses.

Score	Does the writing sample exhibit a good command of language skills?
4	In a Score Point 4 paper, there are no errors that impair the flow of communication. Errors are infrequent and will generally be of the first-draft variety; they have a minor impact on the overall communication. • Do words have very few or no capitalization errors? • Do sentences have very few or no punctuation errors? • Do words have very few or no spelling errors? • Do sentences have very few or no grammar or word usage errors? • Writing has very few or no paragraphing errors. • Writing has very few or no run-on sentences or sentence fragments.
Score	**Does the writing sample exhibit an adequate command of language skills?**
3	In a Score Point 3 paper, errors are occasional but do not impede the flow of communication; the writer's meaning is not seriously obscured by errors in language conventions. • Do words have occasional capitalization errors? • Do sentences have occasional punctuation errors? • Do words have occasional spelling errors? • Do sentences have occasional grammar or word usage errors? • Writing may have occasional paragraphing errors. • Writing may have run-on sentences or sentence fragments.
Score	**Does the writing sample exhibit a minimal command of language skills?**
2	In a Score Point 2 paper, errors are typically frequent and may cause the reader to stop and reread part of the writing. While some aspects of the writing may be more consistently correct than others, the existing errors do impair communication. With a little extra effort on the reader's part, it is still possible to discern most, if not all, of what the writer is trying to communicate. • Do words have frequent capitalization errors? • Do sentences have frequent punctuation errors? • Do words have frequent spelling errors? • Do sentences have frequent grammar or word usage errors? • Writing may have errors in paragraphing, or paragraphing may be missing. • Writing is likely to have run-on sentences or sentence fragments.
Score	**Does the writing sample exhibit a less than minimal command of language skills?**
1	In a Score Point 1 paper, errors are serious and numerous; they often cause the reader to struggle to discern the writer's meaning. Errors are frequently of a wide variety. There may be sections where it is impossible to ascertain what the writer is attempting to communicate. • Do words have many capitalization errors? • Do sentences have many punctuation errors? • Do words have many spelling errors? • Do sentences have many grammar and word usage errors? • Writing may have errors in paragraphing, or paragraphing may be missing. • Writing is likely to have run-on sentences or sentence fragments.

ISTEP+ Extended-Response Writing Applications Overview

This rubric is used to score answers to extended-response questions.

Score	Does the writing sample:
4	• Fully accomplish the task? • Include many relevant ideas? • Organize ideas logically? • Exhibit very good word usage? • Demonstrate very good writing technique? • Demonstrate effective adjustment of language and tone to task and reader?
Score	**Does the writing sample:**
3	• Accomplish the task? • Include relevant ideas? • Organize ideas logically? • Exhibit good word usage? • Demonstrate good writing technique? • Demonstrate an attempt to adjust language and tone to task and reader?
Score	**Does the writing sample:**
2	• Minimally accomplish the task? • Include some relevant ideas? • Exhibit an attempt to organize ideas logically? • Exhibit ordinary word usage? • Demonstrate adequate writing technique? • Demonstrate an attempt to adjust language and tone to task and reader?
Score	**Does the writing sample:**
1	• Only partially accomplish or fail to accomplish the task? • Include few relevant ideas? • Exhibit a minimal attempt to organize ideas logically? • Exhibit minimal word usage? • Demonstrate minimal or less than minimal writing technique? • Demonstrate language and tone that may be inappropriate to task and reader?

ISTEP+ Reading Comprehension Rubric

This rubric is used to score answers to open-ended constructed-response questions.

Score	
2	response includes versions of two exemplars
Score	
1	response includes version of one exemplar
Score	
0	Other

Here is an example of exemplars for an open-ended question:

3 List TWO details from the passage to support the idea that Tito and Bimbo shared a strong, close relationship.

1) _____

   _____

2) _____

   _____

Exemplars:

- As long as people could remember seeing Tito, they had seen Bimbo.
- Tito and Bimbo had been together for twelve or thirteen years.
- Bimbo was Tito's nurse, pillow, playmate, and parents.

Correlations to *ISTEP+* Practice Tests Grade 6

Indiana Academic Standards	Practice Test 1	Practice Test 2	Practice Test 3	Practice Test 4	Practice Test 5
6.1.2 Identify and interpret figurative language.			1	1, 6, 7	5, 7
6.1.4 Use clues to determine meaning of unknown words.		8	11	11	11
6.2.2 Recognize and analyze compare and contrast patterns.	4	5	5	5	10
6.2.3 Clarify main ideas by identifying relationships.	1, 2, 6	7	10	10	9
6.2.4 Clarify understanding with notes, summaries, and graphic organizers.	4, 5, 6	7	9	9	5, 7, 9, 10
6.2.6 Evaluate appropriateness of author's evidence and conclusions.			10, 12	9, 10	9
6.2.7 Make and support conclusions about texts.	2, 3, 4, 5, 6	7	9, 10	9	8, 10
6.2.8 Recognize persuasion, propaganda, and faulty reasoning.			12	12	12

Correlations to *ISTEP+* Practice Tests
Grade 6 *(continued)*

Indiana Academic Standards	Practice Test 1	Practice Test 2	Practice Test 3	Practice Test 4	Practice Test 5
6.3.1 Identify and describe different genres.			5, 12	3	2
6.3.2 Analyze how character affects plot, conflict, and resolution.		2, 3, 5, 6	4	8	8
6.3.3 Analyze affects of setting on plot and resolution.		1	2, 6	6	6
6.3.4 Define how tone and meaning are defined and conveyed in poetry.			1, 3, 5, 6, 7, 8	1, 2, 3, 5	3, 4, 5, 6, 7
6.3.5 Identify speaker, and the difference between points of view.		4	8	2, 4	7
6.3.6 Identify, explain, and interpret theme.		2, 3, 5, 6	1, 4, 5, 6, 7	1, 4, 5, 6, 7	1, 3, 6, 7, 8
6.3.7 Explain effects of literary devices and figurative language.			1, 6, 7	1, 5, 7	3, 4, 5, 7
6.3.8 Evaluate believability of characters and plot.		6	4	8	8

Correlations to *ISTEP+* Practice Tests
Grade 6 *(continued)*

Indiana Academic Standards	Practice Test 1	Practice Test 2	Practice Test 3	Practice Test 4	Practice Test 5
6.4.1 Discuss and maintain a list of ideas.	WP-1, 7	WP-1, 9	WP-1, 13	WP-1, 13	WP-1, 13
6.4.2 Choose form appropriate to purpose.		9	13	13	13
6.4.4 Use appropriate organization.	7	9	13	WP-1, 13	WP-1, 13
6.4.5 Use note-taking skills.			WP-1, 13	WP-1, 13	WP-1, 13
6.4.8 Review, evaluate, and revise for meaning and clarity.	WP-1, 7	WP-1, 9	WP-1, 13	WP-1, 13	WP-1, 13
6.4.9 Use checklist to edit one's own and other's writing.	WP-1, 7	WP-1, 9	WP-1, 13	WP-1, 13	WP-1, 13
6.4.10 Revise writing to improve organization and clarity.	WP-1, 7	WP-1, 9	WP-1, 13	WP-1, 13	WP-1, 13

Correlations to *ISTEP+* Practice Tests
Grade 6 *(continued)*

Indiana Academic Standards	Practice Test 1	Practice Test 2	Practice Test 3	Practice Test 4	Practice Test 5
6.5.1 Write narratives with clear elements, details, and range of devices.	WP-1	WP-1	WP-1	WP-1	WP-1
6.5.4 Write well developed, interpreted, and supported responses to literature.			13	13	13
6.5.5 Write well persuasive compositions with clear purpose and supporting details.	7	9	13	13	13
6.5.6 Use varied word choice.	WP-1, 7	WP-1, 9	WP-1, 13	WP-1, 13	WP-1, 13
6.5.7 Adjust tone and style for purpose and audience.	WP-1, 7	WP-1, 9	WP-1, 13	WP-1, 13	WP-1, 13
6.6.1 Use varied sentence structure.	WP-1, 7	WP-1, 9	WP-1, 13	WP-1, 13	WP-1, 13
6.6.2 Identify and properly use pronouns and verbs.	WP-1, 7	WP-1, 9	WP-1, 13	WP-1, 13	WP-1, 13
6.6.3 Use colons and semi-colons correctly.	WP-1, 7	WP-1, 9	PRAP-1, 13	WP-1, 13	WP-1, 13
6.6.4 Use correct capitalization.	WP-1, 7	WP-1, 9	WP-1, 13	WP-1, 13	WP-1, 13
6.6.5 Spell frequently misspelled words correctly.	WP-1, 7	WP-1, 9	WP-1, 13	WP-1, 13	WP-1, 13

Correlations to *ISTEP+* Practice Tests
Grade 7

Indiana Academic Standards	Practice Test 1	Practice Test 2	Practice Test 3	Practice Test 4	Practice Test 5
7.1.1 Identify idioms, analogies, metaphors, and similes.		2, 8	2	2	2, 5
7.1.2 Use knowledge of Greek, Latin, and Anglo-Saxon roots to understand new words.			12	12	12
7.1.3 Use different strategies to clarify word meaning.		9	12	12	3, 6, 11, 12
7.2.1 Understand and analyze structures of informational materials.			10, 11	8, 9	7, 8, 9
7.2.3 Analyze cause-and-effect organization.			6	4, 6	7
7.2.4 Identify and trace author's viewpoint.	2, 3, 5	6, 7	8, 9, 11	9	8, 9, 10, 11
7.2.6 Assess quality of author's supporting details and recognize bias.		10	11	11	9, 11

Correlations to *ISTEP+* Practice Tests
Grade 7 *(continued)*

Indiana Academic Standards	Practice Test 1	Practice Test 2	Practice Test 3	Practice Test 4	Practice Test 5
7.3.1 Discuss purposes and traits of types of fiction and non-fiction.	1	2, 6, 7	1, 4, 10, 11	8, 9, 10	1, 3
7.3.2 Identify how events advance and foreshadow the plot.	3, 5	1, 6, 7, 10	4, 5, 6, 7	1, 4, 5, 7, 8, 9	4, 5, 7, 8, 9
7.3.3 Analyze characterization.	WP-1, 3, 4, 6	WP-1, 1, 2, 3, 4, 5	WP-1, 3, 5, 6	WP-1, 3, 5, 6, 10	WP-1, 3, 5, 6
7.3.4 Identify and analyze themes.		4	3, 6	3, 4, 5, 10	13
7.4.1 Discuss and maintain a list of ideas for writing.	WP-1, 7	WP-1, 11	WP-1, 13	WP-1, 13	WP-1, 13
7.4.2 Use effective organization and transitions.	WP-1, 7	WP-1, 11	WP-1, 13	WP-1, 13	WP-1, 13
7.4.3 Support statements with appropriate details.	WP-1, 4, 5, 6, 7	WP-1, 4, 5,10, 11	WP-1, 3, 6, 13	WP-1, 3, 11, 13	WP-1, 13
7.4.4 Use brainstorming strategies to determine structure.	WP-1, 7	WP-1, 11	WP-1, 13	WP-1, 13	WP-1, 13
7.4.5 Identify topics; ask valid questions; and develop ideas for research.			WP-1, 13	WP-1, 13	WP-1, 13

Correlations to *ISTEP+* Practice Tests
Grade 7 *(continued)*

Indiana Academic Standards	Practice Test 1	Practice Test 2	Practice Test 3	Practice Test 4	Practice Test 5
7.4.8 Revise writing for clarity.	WP-1, 7	WP-1, 11	WP-1, 13	WP-1, 13	WP-1, 13
7.4.9 Use a checklist to evaluate own and other's writing.	WP-1, 7 11	WP-1, 13	WP-1, 13	WP-1, 13	WP-1,
7.4.10 Revise to improve organization, logic, and word choice.	WP-1, 7 11	WP-1, 13	WP-1, 13	WP-1, 13	WP-1,
7.5.2 Write responses to literature.			13	13	13
7.5.4 Write persuasive compositions.	7	11	13	13	13
7.5.6 Use varied word choice.			WP-1, 13	WP-1, 13	WP-1, 13
7.5.7 Write for different purposes and audiences.	WP-1	WP-1	WP-1	WP-1, 13	WP-1, 13

Correlations to *ISTEP+* Practice Tests
Grade 7 *(continued)*

Indiana Academic Standards	Practice Test 1	Practice Test 2	Practice Test 3	Practice Test 4	Practice Test 5
7.6.1 Appropriately use modifiers and active voice.	WP-1, 7	WP-1, 11	WP-1, 13	WP-1, 13	13
7.6.2 Identify and correctly use infinitives and participles.	WP-1, 7	WP-1,	WP-1,	WP-1,	WP-1,
7.6.3 Make clear references between pronouns and antecedents.	WP-1, 7	WP-1, 11	WP-1, 13	WP-1, 13	WP-1, 13
7.6.5 Demonstrate appropriate English usage.	WP-1, 7	WP-1, 11	WP-1, 13	WP-1, 13	WP-1, 13
7.6.6 Exhibit knowledge of hyphens, dashes, brackets, and semicolons.	WP-1, 7	WP-1, 11	WP-1, 13	WP-1, 13	WP-1, 13
7.6.7 Demonstrate knowledge of quotation marks and commas.	WP-1, 7	WP-1, 11	WP-1, 13	WP-1, 13	WP-1, 13
7.6.8 Use correct capitalization.	WP-1, 7	WP-1, 11	WP-1, 13	WP-1, 13	WP-1, 13
7.6.9 Correctly spell derivates of common base or root words.	WP-1, 7	WP-1, 11	WP-1, 13	WP-1, 13	WP-1, 13

Correlations to *ISTEP+* Practice Tests Grade 8

Indiana Academic Standards	Practice Test 1	Practice Test 2	Practice Test 3	Practice Test 4	Practice Test 5
8.1.1 Analyze and infer meaning of idioms, analogies, similes, and metaphors.		3	5	3, 5, 11	5, 11, 12
8.1.3 Use context clues to verify word meaning.	4	7	5, 7, 11	3	12
8.2.1 Use features of materials to gain meaning.			7	7	7
8.2.2 Analyze text that uses proposition and support patterns.		6, 8, 9	9, 12	11	7, 9, 10
8.2.3 Compare how different texts communicate the same idea.	5		13	13	13
8.2.4 Compare full text to summary to assess accuracy of details.	1	10	3	8, 10, 12	3
8.2.6 Evaluate the logic, internal consistency, and structural patterns of text.	4		8, 10	9	8, 9

Correlations to *ISTEP+* Practice Tests
Grade 8 *(continued)*

Indiana Academic Standards	Practice Test 1	Practice Test 2	Practice Test 3	Practice Test 4	Practice Test 5
8.3.1 Describe purposes and characteristics between different forms of poetry.			4	2, 3	2, 11
8.3.2 Evaluate structural elements of plot and how conflict is resolved.		2, 4, 5	6	9	6
8.3.4 Analyze the affect of setting on text.			1	4	1
8.3.5 Identify and analyze frequently recurring themes.			3	1	6
8.3.6 Identify metaphor, symbolism, dialect and irony and interpret their affect on the work.		1, 3	1, 4	3, 4, 5, 6, 11	1, 4
8.3.7 Explain how a work reflects the author's background.			2, 3, 6	2, 7	3, 10

Correlations to *ISTEP+* Practice Tests
Grade 8 *(continued)*

Indiana Academic Standards	Practice Test 1	Practice Test 2	Practice Test 3	Practice Test 4	Practice Test 5
8.4.1 Discuss and maintain a list of ideas for writing.	WP-1	WP-1	WP-1	WP-1	WP-1
8.4.2 Create compositions with a clear, well supported thesis and conclusion.	WP-1, 7	WP-1, 11	WP-1, 13	WP-1, 13	WP-1, 13
8.4.3 Support theses with appropriate evidence.	2, 3, 6, 7	11	13	13	WP-1
8.4.7 Revise writing for clarity.	WP-1, 7	WP-1, 11	WP-1, 13	WP-1, 13	WP-1, 13
8.4.8 Use a checklist to evaluate one's own and other's writing.	WP-1, 7	WP-1, 11	WP-1, 13	WP-1, 13	WP-1, 13
8.4.9 Revise writing to strengthen vocabulary, structure, and clarity.	WP-1, 7	WP-1, 11	WP-1, 13	WP-1, 13	WP-1, 13

Correlations to *ISTEP+* Practice Tests
Grade 8 *(continued)*

Indiana Academic Standards	Practice Test 1	Practice Test 2	Practice Test 3	Practice Test 4	Practice Test 5
8.5.1 Write biographies, autobiographies, and short stories.			WP-1	WP-1	WP-1
8.5.3 Write well supported research reports with clear thesis and organization.			13	13	13
8.5.4 Write persuasive compositions with clear thesis and logical supporting evidence.	7	WP-1, 11	13	13	13
8.5.6 Use precise word choice.	WP-1, 7	WP-1, 11	WP-1, 13	WP-1, 13	WP-1, 13
8.5.7 Adjust style and tone for purpose and audience.	WP-1, 7	WP-1, 11	WP-1, 13	WP-1, 13	WP-1, 13
8.6.1 Use correct and varied sentence types.	WP-1, 7	WP-1, 11	WP-1, 13	WP-1	WP-1, 13
8.6.4 Edit to correct grammar.	WP-1, 7	WP-1, 11	WP-1, 13	WP-1, 13	WP-1, 13
8.6.5 Use correct punctuation.	WP-1, 7	WP-1, 11	PRAP-1, 13	WP-1, 13	WP-1, 13
8.6.6 Use correct capitalization.	WP-1, 7	WP-1, 11	WP-1, 13	WP-1, 13	WP-1, 13
8.6.7 Use correct spelling conventions.	WP-1, 7	WP-1, 11	WP-1, 13	WP-1, 13	WP-1, 13

ISTEP+ ANSWER KEY Grade 6

page 3

2. expression

3. consisting of two parts

page 5

2. a small piece or part that is broken off

3. fracture

page 7

2. **Exemplars:** Simile: "half-grown chrysanthemums…like accusers"; the flowers are "staring up" toward the speaker like an accuser would; Simile: "line of elms…like horses"; the elm trees are moving around like horses do

3. **Exemplars:** the wind bellows; flowers stare up like accusers; elms plunge and toss

page 9

2. She compares and contrasts the instruments in all three paragraphs.

3. Woodwinds and brass instruments can be used in many different musical groups.

page 11

2. Main Idea: Tito is a blind orphan who is never seen without Bimbo by his side. **Exemplars:** They didn't live anywhere. He was blind—had been blind since birth. As long as people could remember seeing Tito, they had seen Bimbo.

3. **Exemplars:** As long as people could remember seeing Tito, they had seen Bimbo. Tito and Bimbo had been together for twelve or thirteen years. Bimbo was Tito's nurse, pillow, playmate, and parents.

page 13

2. After the ice storms of December 28 and 29, the trees and buildings around town looked as pretty as they ever have.

3. People in this part of the state are not especially fond of these types of storms.

page 15

2. Conclusion: Loch Ness is a large and mysterious body of water. **Exemplars:** Underwater…were deep hidden ravines, rocky canyons and caves…dark recesses far below the surface. One earlier investigator heard strange underwater sounds…sounds that no biologist has yet been able to successfully identify.

3. **Exemplars:** The research team was excited about the newly-discovered underwater features. An investigator was in the area a year earlier and heard strange sounds.

page 17

2. fiction

3. a few characters and themes in a single narrative

page 19

2. "he felt that he must do something"

3. an unnamed third-person narrator

page 21

2. The designers of the Internet faced many challenging problems.

3. scorekeeping methods in different games

page 23

2. By exploring the world, a person can experience joy, freedom, and possibility.

3. travel the open road

page 25

2. He wants to stay home from school.

3. morning

pages 26–35

1. the long history of the Abenaki in places now called New England and Canada

2. describe various parts of traditional Abenaki life

3. The Abenaki traded with the Europeans.

4. Two things being compared: Abenaki in New England and Canada in past centuries and Abenaki in New England and Canada today; **Exemplars:** Alike: Native Americans living among non-Native Americans in New England and Canada; interested in traditional activities; Different: before Europeans, Abenaki lived as they wished; today Abenaki's land, rights, traditions reduced by non-Native Americans

5. destructive; **Exemplars:** The Abenaki lost most of their land to the Europeans; European diseases killed many Abenaki

6. **Exemplars:** fished rivers in spring and autumn, farmed corn and other crops, hunted animals in forests

7. Students should write a persuasive essay, using details from the passage to support their views.

pages 37–39

1. Langston's accomplishments as an African-American statesman

2. Langston was one of the first African Americans to serve in Congress.

3. protect

4. **Exemplars:** lawyer: organized societies to find legal ways to help African Americans; political leader: he was a U.S. diplomat; he served in U.S. Congress

5. empathy; **Exemplars:** Forming anti-slavery societies showed Langston's sense of empathy. After the Civil War, Langston empathized with the hardships of freed slaves and sought to help them; justice: **Exemplars:** Langston sought justice in the form of freedom for enslaved African Americans. After slavery was outlawed, Langston worked to help African Americans find work, shelter, and freedom from poverty, which he believed was rightfully theirs.

6. **Exemplars:** Before Civil War: Langston was born in1829 as a free African American in Virginia; in 1834, he was sent with his brothers to Ohio; Langston excelled in giving speeches and studied law at Oberlin College; he formed anti-slavery societies; he used home for Underground Railroad. After Civil War: Langston helped newly-freed slaves avoid hardships; he served as U.S. diplomat to Haiti; in 1889, he was elected to U.S. Congress

7. believed in serving the needs of people less fortunate than himself

8. took

9. Students should write a persuasive essay, using details from the passage to support their views.

pages 40–42

1. Why is the sun dangerous?

2. If unprotected skin is exposed to ultraviolet rays, it can turn red, burn, and hurt.

3. harm your skin

4. **Exemplars:** skin turns red, skin burns, skin hurts, damaged skin may begin to peel, peeling leaves a new layer of skin that is unhealthy, thin, and sensitive

5. to inform people about the sun's dangers: **Exemplars:** The author provides specific information about the effects of ultraviolet rays on the skin. The author informs the reader about the long-term effects of sunburned skin; to persuade people to use sunscreen: **Exemplars:** The author uses a variety of facts about the benefits of sunscreen in order to persuade readers to use it to protect their skin. The author tries to persuade people to wear sunscreen by explaining that experts such as doctors recommend its use.

6. Though you may like to get a tan, exposure to the sun's ultraviolet rays will damage your skin.

7. protegere

8. harm

9. Students should write an essay persuading peers to make healthy choices.

pages 43–45

1. The narration is third person, from the perspective of an unnamed narrator.

2. It creates a sense of comfort and protection because Jenny and the cat are safe and dry in her home.

3. caring

4. In fact, the cat was almost ugly, with dirty paws and a white coat that had yellowed slightly, like an old newspaper.

5. being thoughtful: **Exemplars:** Jenny can't stop thinking about the cat all week; Jenny realizes that she loves the cat; taking initiative: **Exemplars:** Jenny brings food to the cat, Jenny takes the cat home with her

6. **Exemplars:** Looks: The cat has dirty paws and its fur is yellowing. Behaves: The cat seems to watch the world with amusement.

7. Jenny finds the cat in the pouring rain.

8. a short story

9. Students should write an essay evaluating the believability of the story, using details from the passage to support their views.

pages 47–61

1. Victor does not live on a farm.

2. He wants to help his uncle.

3. She often starts conflicts with others and tries to get away from the herd.

4. An unnamed third-person narrator tells the story.

5. **Exemplars:** Victor's views about goats at the beginning: "made Victor uncomfortable to be around so many strange creatures"; "goats were the strangest"; "bizarre bleating sounds"; "tried to refuse because he thought watching the goats was too scary"; Victor's views about goats at the end: "smiled as he thought of the runaway"; "Had he actually enjoyed his adventure"; "laughed to himself with satisfaction"; "wasn't afraid of goats anymore"

6. **Exemplars:** loses fear of goats: throws arms around Lechuga's neck and carries her

back; laughs to himself and realizes his fear is gone; learns responsibility: takes care of "one ram, three nannies, and two kids"; figures out how to get back to the farm and carries Lechuga back to rest of herd

7. **Exemplars:** Agriculture in the U.S. before the 1940s: Different fruits and vegetables appeared in stores in different seasons. Agriculture in the U.S. after the 1940s: Fruits and vegetables are available all year.

8. tougher

9. Students should write a persuasive letter, using details from the passage to support their views.

pages 63–82

1. hearing

2. a farm in late summer

3. laughing corn

4. celebrating the ways of nature and harvest time

5. **Exemplars:** What is being compared: the farmer and his wife and the wind and the corn and the rain and the sun; Alike: both "talk things over together"; both work together to accomplish things; Different: farmer and wife are human, whereas corn is a vegetable and wind, rain, sun are elements of nature; human literally talk, parts of nature do not literally talk

6. the importance of the harvest

7. **Exemplars:** corn and wind/laughter/line 7; birds/blackbirds are hoarse/line 8; birds/one of the smaller blackbirds chitters/line 9; wind and corn/The wind and the corn talk/line 16; rain, corn/the rain and the corn . . . talk/lines 17–18; farmer, wife/The farmer and his wife talk/line 22

8. **Exemplars:** serious: Sandburg uses words like "fooling" and "laughter," but his speaker isn't trying to be funny. Sandburg's focus on tiny details such as "white juice" and "cornsilk creeps in the end" shows that his speaker takes the subject seriously.

admiring: Sandburg uses language such as "majestic" and "conquering" that gives a sense of importance to the crop. In line 15, the speaker's forcefulness ("Always—I never knew it any other way") shows admiration for the ways of nature.

9. **Exemplars:** what type of bird; how old bird is; whether it is male or female

10. **Exemplars:** Bird-watching is considered a "serious" hobby by people who spend a great deal of time and care identifying and observing birds and recording details about their appearance and behavior. Some scientists are serious about bird-watching, because they use information gathered by birders to expand their own research.

11. simple

12. Some of the most interesting birds that birders observe are predators.

13. Students should write a persuasive letter, using details from the passage to support their views.

pages 83–102

1. short-lived
2. sorrowful
3. AAABB
4. The speaker is in conflict with the passage of time.
5. **Exemplars:** "That my days have been a dream" or "all that we see or seem/Is but a dream within a dream"; the poet seems to say that our lives and our hopes are as temporary and fleeting as dreams.
6. hopelessness
7. **Exemplars:** the grains of golden sands symbolize time; the pitiless wave symbolizes death
8. **Exemplars:** agitated and sad: The speaker weeps while watching grains of sand slip away from his or her grasp; the speaker exclaims two rhetorical questions about his or her powerlessness in the face of death.
9. **Exemplars:** Loss of habitat isn't the only problem caused by development.

10. **Exemplars:** The amount of panther habitat is shrinking. Panthers are dying as they attempt to cross an increasing number of roads in the region.

11. problems

12. Therefore, experts must plan ahead and set aside one or two large protected areas where panthers can live, rather than many smaller areas.

13. Students should write a persuasive essay, using details from the passage to support their views.

pages 103–122

1. the importance of military strength
2. slant rhyme
3. evening
4. simile
5. **Exemplars:** sorrowful: "Dark hills at evening"; "sunset hovers like a sound/Of golden horns that sang to rest"; " You fade—as if the last of days were fading"
6. Soldiers who once lived are now dead.
7. **Exemplars:** days: "as if the last of days/ Were fading"; wars: "all wars were done"
8. **Exemplars:** pity: the soldiers are now nothing more than bones; the soldiers' accomplishments are overshadowed by their deaths. admiration: the soldiers acted with bravery while they were alive; their lives and accomplishments are still celebrated with "golden horns."
9. Athletes spend extra time on physical activity and less time studying.
10. **Exemplars:** Athletes may exhaust or injure themselves if they take part in team sports as well as P.E. courses. Student athletes could use the time ordinarily spent in P.E. courses to study.
11. allow
12. Finally, as I understand it, P.E. courses are supposed to develop an interest in athletics.

13. Students should write a persuasive essay, using details from the passage to support their views.

page 124

1. the author's name

2. Doris will lose interest in the puppy.

3. **Exemplars:** puppies: Most puppies are cute and lovable. Detail: "about six months old"; Prediction: Doris's parents will become fond of the puppy; children and adults in a family: Adults make the big decisions. Detail: Doris "knew her parents wouldn't let her keep it"; Prediction: Doris won't be able to make the final decision about keeping the puppy

page 125

1. Becky and her mother

2. **Exemplars:** Point of view: first-person; Example: "Over and over I told my mum I wanted a bike."

page 126

1. dictionary

2. *-vis-*

3. primarily

4. *-ver-*

page 127

1. Webster was responsible for all people speaking the same language.

2. The Blue-Backed Speller sold nearly 100 million copies.

3. Underlined details might include *most valuable and any American ever did*. Noah Webster's dictionary is an example of American scholarship.

page 128

1. Mark Twain's hair is not too thick or too long.

2. **Exemplars:** just right, greatly improves the beauty of his features, wonderfully shaped head and profile, extraordinarily fine

looking man, the loveliest man I ever saw or ever hope to see

3. Students should write an essay using an enthusiastic tone.

page 129

1. probation

2. probe

3. factor

4. faction

page 130

1. is sitting in the tree out of fear

2. Paul

3. **Exemplars:** sitting in apple tree alone; white with fear; carved anxious warning in tree bark

page 131

1. Janet and Richard disagree about whether Janet should play on Richard's baseball team.

2. **Exemplars:** Similar: both used to be friends with one another; both are angry at each other; both like to play baseball; both want the other person to return something of theirs; both hope that something bad happens to other person; Different: Richard doesn't think girls should play on the baseball team, while Janet wants to play

page 132

1. ferry

2. speculated

3. spectacle

4. transfer

page 133

1. Kwan Ming's family was poor.

2. Conclusion: The voyage to the New World was long and difficult. **Exemplars:** lasted six weeks; rocky waves, screaming storms; huddled together with hundreds of other Chinese deep in the ship's hold

page 134

1. Nature is powerful and impossible to control.

2. **Exemplars:** Time: dusk; autumn sun sinking; Place: the station; dark, frozen plain; broad and endless; plain merged with the sky; darkening space; a village; still, cold, frosty

3. Students should write an essay persuading the trip's organizers to consider—or to rule out—rural Russia as a destination.

page 135

1. eventually
2. believable
3. reasonable
4. widely

page 136

1. to inform

2. **Exemplars:** It was 1945, and World War II had ended. (fact; to inform); Americans of all races had died for their country. (fact; to inform); Yet black men were still not allowed in the major leagues. (fact; to inform); Branch Rickey of the Brooklyn Dodgers thought that was wrong. (fact; to inform); He was the only team owner who believed blacks and whites should play together. (fact; to inform)

page 137

1. autobiography

2. **Exemplars:** Uses pronoun *I*: "I did not know this until afterward"; "When I had played with it a little while…"; "I was at once interested in this finger play…"; "When I finally succeeded in making the letters correctly, I was flushed…" "Running downstairs to my mother I held up my hand…" "I did not know that I was spelling a word…"; "I was simply…"; Explains author's actions or gives insights into events: "I was at once interested in this finger play and tried to imitate it."; "I was

flushed with pleasure and pride."; "I did not know that I was spelling a word or even that words existed."

page 138

1. connection
2. accomplishment
3. imitation
4. astonishment

page 139

1. What point of view does the author use in this selection?

2. Frederick Douglass realizes that literacy brings freedom.

3. **Exemplars:** Mrs. Auld: the alphabet, spelling, reading; Mr. Auld: the power of reading and knowledge, the connection between knowledge and freedom

page 140

1. earnest

2. **Exemplars:** "sheep's wool was faded"; "full of odor and resin"; "precious idea"

page 141

1. something that provides a solution or an explanation

2. used something as the starting point for something else

3. to supply

page 142

1. not tamed
2. encircling
3. isolating

4. **Exemplars:** "marshmallows"; "springs"; "tennis shoes"; "what boys needed and wanted"

page 143

1. golden

2. **Exemplars:** "Yet he will find a chink or two/To slip his golden fingers through";

"Meantime his golden face around/He bares to all the garden ground,"; "The gardener of the World, he goes."

3. Students should write an essay that evaluates the poet's use of sound devices and imagery, using details from the poem to support their ideas.

page 144

1. precaution
2. preview
3. restore
4. recycling

page 145

1. The brothers show more loyalty toward each other than any other brothers.
2. **Exemplars:** It shan't: It shall not; It won't; It will not; Praised each other's daring: complimented each other on his bravery

page 146

1. repetition
2. **Exemplars:** repetition: at all, at all, at all; alliteration: busy beetle; onomatopoeia: tap-tapping

page 147

1. unexpectedly precious
2. simple and straightforward
3. trouble

page 148

1. specific details
2. the fact that Jay becomes interested in an unusual pair of boots
3. **Exemplars:** Jay bored at home; Joan looks for outfit to wear on date; Joan says they must go shopping; Jay disappointed seeing thrift store instead of mall; Jay attracted by old shoes; Joan finds dress and Jay boots to buy; Jay eager to tell friends about boots and thrift store

page 149

1. stage directions
2. **Exemplars:** It tells me that Milo is polite; It tells me where the characters will go next.
3. Students should write an essay that explains the function of dialogue in plays.

page 150

1. brevity
2. inscription
3. abbreviate
4. invisible

page 151

1. Carter is upset; Amber is annoyed.
2. They are related to one another.
3. **Exemplars:** At first, Amber is frustrated a little hostile to her brother. Later, Amber is still frustrated with her brother but she feels bad about how she's acted.

page 152

1. the words *This is the numbers mine*
2. **Exemplars:** Help readers picture props, costumes, or lighting: "LIGHTS UP A LITTLE"; Help readers picture action in the play: "Little Men digging and chopping, shoveling and scraping"; Help readers picture setting and scenery: "Iridescent and glittery numbers seem to sparkle from everywhere."
3. Students should write an explanatory essay that includes details to convey a particular mood.

page 153

1. a paved outdoor area next to a house
2. a meeting at an appointed place and time
3. a round thin cake of cornmeal or wheat flour bread

page 154

1. he and his wife have no child
2. because he does so most every day

3. **Exemplars:** his wife will know his grief; his wife's grief will be doubled

page 155

1. was trapped in the underworld

2. **Exemplars:** mortal: Orpheus marries a mortal and decides to follow her to the underworld after her death; this would not be such a momentous decision if Orpheus were a god. Orpheus notes that "no mortal has ever been" to the underworld, but says that he must do it; this suggests that he is a mortal himself.

3. Students should write a persuasive speech using at least two details from the passage.

page 156

1. result

2. reason

3. effect

4. cause

page 157

1. creating a detailed outline of the ideas in the passage

2. **Exemplars:** Purpose: learning about ancient Greek culture; Clues: Greek names in the title; island of Crete; King Minos; Minotaur and the labyrinth

page 158

1. False rumors can destroy relationships between individuals.

2. **Exemplars:** lion: "a plan began to form in the lion's mind"; "secretly he started spreading evil and slanderous reports"; "exactly what the lion wanted"; bulls: "distrustingly, began to avoid one another"

3. Students should write an essay that persuades the bulls of the coming danger, using details from the passage to support their main idea.

page 159

1. quiet

2. unknown

3. messy

4. fantastic

ISTEP+ ANSWER KEY Grade 7

page 3

2. **Exemplars:** have a four-chambered heart; breathe air through lungs; even have hair when born

3. **Exemplars:** whales are the only mammals; to life in the ocean

page 5

2. into

3. painful

page 7

2. metaphor

3. And like lovely notes in a serenade to the stars, they fly by night.

page 9

2. India

3. poetry

page 11

2. Rudi rescues a famous mountain climber.

3. "foremost mountaineer" and "pull him from a crevasse—save him"

page 13

2. **Exemplars:** Fact: When magma reaches the Earth's surface it is called lava. Opinion: Volcanoes are very interesting to study.

3. **Exemplars:** Facts: A volcano is a place in the Earth's surface through which melting rock and other materials reach the surface. Deep within the Earth, under exceptional pressure and extreme temperatures, rock exists in the form of hot liquid called *magma*. When magma reaches the Earth's surface it is called *lava*. Kilauea, on the Island of Hawaii, is a volcano with active lava flows. Explanation: All of these statements can be proved, so they are facts. Opinions: Volcanoes are very

interesting to study. In order to get a sense of a volcano's power, it is best to visit one and see the flows from up close. Indeed, Kilauea is simply a marvel! Explanation: These statements all contain personal feelings and cannot be proved, so they are opinions.

page 15

2. **Exemplars:** Sarah is brave because she dives into the sea even though she has never dived off a cliff before. Jenny is not as brave as Sarah because she gets nervous as she watches Jenny dive off the cliff.

3. **Exemplars:** Conclusion: The passage is set in Mexico. Examples: The girls gaze down into the Gulf of Mexico. They had watched the local Mexican children diving off the cliffs.

page 17

2. nonfiction

3. short stories and a play

page **19**

2. from a first-person point of view

3. an old man

page 21

2. People overreact at illness and end up taking up valuable time from their doctors.

3. facts and opinions

page 23

2. the pain of separation and loneliness

3. When I go away from you/The world beats dead

page 25

2. a school gym

3. a dreamer

pages 31–35

1. narrative

2. The author uses the seasons to structure the body of the text.

3. picture what Justin saw on his hike

4. **Exemplars:** has a detailed memory: Justin remembers how the pool water feels against his skin on hot summer days; he remembers picnics and ballgames in the summer; he remembers the way autumn leaves produce a special orange-yellow light; he remembers sitting in his basement with friends; he remembers the ice and snow of the winter; he remembers the balmy afternoons of spring when he begged his mother to let him stay outside; he remembers planting a garden; he remembers hiking with his friends.

5. **Exemplars:** Alike: Spring and summer are relatively warm; you can play outside in the spring and summer; it stays light later in the day in both seasons; Different: Summer is usually warmer than spring

6. **Exemplars:** Summer: He remembered the blessed feeling of the cool water against his hot skin and how refreshing that was. He remembered catching fireflies on warm early-summer nights. Autumn: The brightly colored leaves produced a special orange-yellow light. Justin remembered raking them into pile and letting the young neighborhood children fumble their way through them, falling into the piles with glee. He remembered sitting in his basement with his friends, telling scary Halloween stories and with only the flicker of candles to light the room. Winter: He remembered the muffled sounds of traffic after a thick snowfall blanketed the streets. Spring: He took great enjoyment in remembering the first balmy afternoons when the sun set just a little later every day. Best of all, he hiked with his friends along wooded streams and watched as the gush of water from the melting snow swelled the rushing brooks.

7. Students should take a position by choosing a favorite season, using details from the passage to support their views.

pages 37–39

1. To read poetry is leads to self-discovery and a new way to experience one's reality.

2. analogy

3. imagination; **Exemplars:** different people have lived under it, lived with it, responded to it; poetry brings a special spell to the fact of the sun

4. **Exemplars:** a handful of gravel; an ice cube

5. responded

6. **Exemplars:** body; blood; muscles

7. ownership

8. Encountering poetry for the first time requires a personal journey within and a willingness to open oneself to new ways of experiencing one's surroundings.

pages 40–42

1. simile

2. Homer was single-minded, driven, and a self-taught genius.

3. good-natured

4. **Exemplars:** Before Tynemouth: He only took five painting lessons. His work included more women, children, and country life. He considered the sea to be serene. At Tynemouth: He thought more critically about his own life and work. The subjects of most of his paintings showed the harsh existence of men of the sea. The sea became a powerful force of nature to him.

5. inspirational; **Exemplars:** The people of Tynemouth, especially the men of the sea, were heroic, and to Homer, represented the best example of mankind. Watching them live their difficult lives made him think critically about his own life and work. Instead of simply serene, the sea had become a powerful force of nature to him.

6. grumpy

7. **Exemplars:** the harsh reality of people's struggles against the sea, the heroism of men and women, the sea as a force of nature

8. to inform

9. Students should write a persuasive essay to a local museum and include versions of two exemplars. **Exemplars:** His oil paintings and watercolors are in all major American museums today. But even when Winslow Hunter was alive, they called him America's greatest painter.

pages 43–45

1. The boy and his mother walk to school.

2. It is first-person narration, told from the boy's point of view.

3. The boy and his mother are making sure they do everything correctly to get him enrolled in school.

4. understand the feelings of the narrator

5. **Exemplars:** Circumstances: He speaks little English when he first enrolls in school. He's of Mexican heritage. Emotions: He's nervous at first, and he and his mother rehearse before meeting the principal. He wants to be accepted for who he is.

6. **Exemplars:** superstructure, firm shoulders, thin lips that moved like steel springs, not a giant in body but when she mobilized it to a standing position she seemed a match for giants

7. fair; **Exemplars:** Her eyes a warm welcome and she smiled. Miss Hopley encouraged the narrator to become a proud American without punishing him for speaking his native language.

8. not denying his heritage

9. Students should write a persuasive letter to their friends and include versions of two exemplars. **Exemplars:** I noticed other differences, none of them reassuring. No one was ever punished for speaking in his native tongue on the playground. It was easy for me to feel that becoming a proud American.

pages 53–61

1. Mira goes into the garden.

2. personification

3. It was her sixteenth birthday.

4. **Exemplars:** Similar: Both Mira and Vanity enjoy looking at themselves in the mirror. They are both wearing fancy clothing. Differences: Vanity does not tell the truth, while Mira does not seem to be a liar.

5. conceited; **Exemplars:** She believes she is the most beautiful in the village. She spends all of her time looking at her image in the mirror. She trusts the image reflected in Vanity's mirror and can only love and gaze upon herself.

6. A workable partnership between plants and animals allows for the balance of nature and, ultimately, the survival of our planet.

7. 2

8. an analogy

9. move into

10. **Exemplars:** ocean; reason: Whales were almost destroyed by excessive hunting; forest; reasons: Humans and logging are taking over more and more forest and putting the animals that live there at risk.

11. Students should write a persuasive essay about the preservation of animal habitats, using details from the passage to support their views.

pages 71–82

1. the moral

2. an analogy

3. wise; **Exemplars:** "A cold winter is coming. You had better get busy storing up some food for the days ahead." "It will help me keep warm during the cold days of winter." busy; **Exemplars:** The ant was sweating and working very hard. The tiny insect was busily dragging an entire ear of corn down the road. The grasshopper awoke from a pleasant nap only to find the ant dragging a huge chunk of rabbit fur down the road.

4. animals as characters

5. understand the difference between the two characters

6. **Exemplars:** Sometimes, as he sang a song, he also hopped about, doing a dance to celebrate the easy life of summer. The grasshopper laughed and said, "Look around you, there is plenty to eat." "My hammock and shady home are just perfect," he bragged.

7. Galileo invents the telescope.

8. Space probes that orbit other planets can teach us much about those planets and may teach us more about our own.

9. 3 and 4

10. **Exemplars:** Alike: both have gone into space, both have collected data about our universe; Different: early probes could only fly by planets, but newer probes can orbit planets, newer probes can land on planets

11. mostly facts; **Exemplars:** The Hubble space telescope, for example, orbits above the Earth's atmosphere. Planets in the inner solar system were studied by *Viking* orbiters at Mars and the *Magellan* orbiter at Venus. *Galileo* was launched in 1989 and reached Jupiter in 1995.

12. forefront

13. Students should write a persuasive essay arguing either for or against continued funding for space travel and research, using details from the passage to support their views.

pages 91–102

1. on a rock

2. a simile

3. vanity and vengeance; Exemplary: "Some time ago, my mother, proud of her beauty and of mine, dared to say that we were more beautiful than the sea nymphs." "Enraged, they went to Poseidon, the god of the sea, and demanded vengeance for my mother's insult." "The oracle told my father that the only way to stop the

destruction was to offer me as a sacrifice to the sea monster."

4. Perseus will continue to perform heroic deeds.

5. understand that Perseus has already performed a very heroic deed

6. **Exemplars:** Hermes, a god, gives him wings to help him fly and a cap that makes him invisible; he defeats two very strong and dangerous opponents: Medusa and the sea monster.

7. the present

8. The USDA Beagle Brigade will continue to be used to protect U.S. agriculture.

9. Beagles like Junior help protect U.S. agriculture from foreign pests and diseases.

10. **Exemplars:** He and the 60 other dogs in the USDA's Beagle Brigade cruise international airports across the country in search of forbidden fruit, vegetables, plants, and meat. Across the country, the Beagles and their handlers are responsible for about 60,000 seizures of prohibited agricultural products yearly.

11. fact; **Exemplars:** Many international travelers don't realize that even a single piece of fruit packed in a suitcase has the potential to unleash a pest that could devastate U.S. crops. Across the country, the Beagles and their handlers are responsible for about 60,000 seizures of prohibited agricultural products yearly.

12. allowed

13. Students should write a persuasive essay arguing either for or against a Beagle Brigade presence in the town.

pages 111–122

1. on the island of Crete

2. a simile

3. foolish; **Exemplars:** For Icarus, these cautions went in at one ear and out by the other. And not an idea remained in the boy's head but the one joy of escape.

4. Icarus will get into some trouble as he flies.

5. picture Daedalus learning to fly

6. **Exemplars:** He built a Labyrinth so cunning that one needed a magic clue to get through. He built a pair of wings that allowed him to fly.

7. An avalanche of ice comes crashing down.

8. Climbs like this are extremely dangerous, but also beautiful.

9. It gives an example of the dangers of the climb.

10. **Exemplars:** man vs. nature: avalanching ice, glacier's movements, melting ice and snow; man vs. self: "After waiting a few minutes to regain my composure", "forgot to be afraid"

11. excitement and fear; **Exemplars:** "But if the icefall was strenuous and terrifying, it had a surprising allure as well. As dawn washed the darkness from the sky, the shattered glacier was revealed to be a three-dimensional landscape of phantasmal beauty." "I froze, my heart in my throat, but the avalanching ice passed fifty yards to the left, out of sight, without doing any damage. After waiting a few minutes to regain my composure I resumed my herky-jerky passage to the far side of the ladder."

12. ice mass

13. Students should write a persuasive essay arguing either for or against the sport of mountain climbing.

page 124

1. for appearance rather than for use

2. clothes

3. **Exemplars:** our hero-worshipping; backwards; the men who had *caused* the need for bandages

page 125

1. third-person omniscient

2. **Exemplars:** she remembered the sun and the way the sun was and the sky was when she was four in Ohio; they had been on Venus all their lives, and they had…long since forgotten the color and heat of it; And so, the children hated her for all these reasons of big and little consequence

3. Students should write an essay that explores how the story might be different if it were told from another point of view, using details from the passage to support their views.

page 126

1. listeners at an event

2. militant

3. sensational

4. glorious

page 127

1. to inform

2. **Exemplars:** Paragraph 2: Main Idea: About half of the population were farmers, but most people relied on food from outside the city. Purpose: The purpose of the paragraph is to describe the people that lived in the city. Paragraph 3: Main Idea: Large houses and palaces in the center of the city were made of adobe and whitewashed. Purpose: The purpose of this paragraph is to describe what homes and dwellings looked like in Tenochtitlan.

page 128

1. to find out information about his ancestors

2. **Exemplars:** slavery, the Civil War

3. Students should write an essay analyzing how the historical context affects the author's actions, using details from the passage to support their views.

page 129

1. not

2. before

3. not

4. to cause by force

page 130

1. He will try to learn more about the old man and his treasure.

2. respect; **Exemplars:** He was an old man; [Greg] had seen him before, picking through trash on the corner; "You ain't one of them bad boys looking for my treasure is you?"; "Every man got a treasure. You don't know that, you must be a fool!"

page 131

1. He has great respect and admiration for the old man.

2. **Exemplars:** The bird flies out of the old man's hand; the bird suspends itself in space; the bird scares the life out of the narrator

page 132

1. skill or talent

2. variety

3. picture

page 133

1. an injured cat

2. **Exemplars:** Inference: The narrator is a vet. Details: I was finishing the evening surgery; He had no animal with him.

page 134

1. Felix and Antonio are fighting in a boxing ring.

2. The two boxers rush toward each other and embrace.

3. Students should write an essay exploring the theme of the story, using details from the passage to support their views.

page 135

1. not easily forgotten

2. move away

3. in or towards

page 136

1. Mr. Peters and the swans shared a very special connection.

2. **Exemplars:** people used to say that he talked to swans and they understood him; he would not think of moving to a drier spot, but went slowly about his work, with the two swans always somewhere close at hand; passers-by along the road heard the mournful sound of two swans singing the night Mr. Peters died

page 137

1. It presents facts and explains the events that led to the invention of Band-Aids®.

2. **Exemplars:** Conclusion: Earle Dickson was a talented and creative man.

page 138

1. out or outside of

2. beyond normal

3. together

4. no longer existing

page 139

1. Corn and vegetables have been the basic food ingredients in Mexico for thousands of years.

2. **Exemplars:** Facts: The Mexican fishing industry has greatly expanded in recent years, growing from a catch of about 390,000 tons ten years ago to a catch of about 800,000 tons today; Up to now, fish hasn't been consumed in large quantities in Mexicoævegetables such as corn and beans have been basic the ingredients here for thousands of years; My work as a marine biologist concentrates on the marine turtle; This animal is common in tropical waters the world over, and of the eight species that are known to exist, seven can be found in the waters off both the east and west coasts of Mexico; Opinions: But I believe Mexico is now overpopulated and in the near future will rely more and more on the sea for its food; I feel the world should be more conscious of the marine environment and do more to help conserve the turtle, and other endangered species.

page 140

1. Prejudice can be learned and unlearned.

2. **Exemplars:** the task of bringing us all together can be accomplished by government; parents can help to create a tolerant society; we can put our faith in young people as a positive force; babies come into this world as blank slates and, with their beautiful innocence, see others not as different but as enjoyable companions

3. Students should write an essay that explains the meaning of the phrase and tells whether they agree with the author or not, using details from the passage to support their views.

page 141

1. an artistic dance form performed to music

2. a truck or vehicle

3. an expression or phrase

page 142

1. Suzy and Leah will become good friends.

2. **Exemplars:** Conclusion: Leah lost relatives to the Nazis; Leah does not trust Suzy; Details: Leah writes that she expects Suzy will stop being nice to her, like the German; Suzy reads Leah diary and learns that her relatives were killed.

page 143

1. a simile

2. Students should write an essay that describes how the poet uses figurative language to bring the blacksmith to life, using examples from the poem to support their views.

page 144

1. in

2. heart

3. air

page 145

1. I would have to cut his beard as I did with any other customer, being careful not to cut him.

2. **Exemplars:** Though I was a revolutionary in secret, I took my job as barber very seriously.

page 146

1. The ends of the second and fourth lines in each stanza rhyme.

2. **Exemplars:** Alliteration: The day is done, and the darkness; Explanation: Alliteration is the repetition of a consonant sound at the beginning of words in a line of poetry. In this line from the poem, the poet repeats the *d* at beginning of *day*, *done*, and *darkness*.

page 147

1. high-quality

2. quest for

3. installed

4. motivation

page 148

1. The T1100 Deluxe has many great features.

2. in an advertisement

3. **Exemplars:** Purpose: to learn more about the T1100 Deluxe washing machine; Details: With five speed settings, the T1100 can handle your heaviest denims and your most delicate hand-washable fabrics; Your Windmark T1100 Deluxe is covered under warranty for ten years after the purchase of the machine.

page 149

1. the way characters deliver their dialogue

2. **Exemplars:** Holmes: clever; "I…I knew you caused Victor Savage's death"; Smith: menacing; "[*Snarling*] Did you? Well proving it is a different matter, Holmes"

3. Students should write an essay explaining what the stage directions tell them about the character of Smith, using examples from the passage to support their views.

page 150

1. established pattern of action or thought
2. adverb
3. full of

page 151

1. Alyce was knocked down by a ewe as she washed its face in the cool river.
2. **Exemplars:** the river had been dammed up to form a washing pool; Edward soon took on the job of matching mothers and babies.

page 152

1. He's keeping a date made with a friend twenty years before.
2. Bob does not recognize the man at first. Bob tells the man how much he has changed.
3. Students should write an essay that explores Jimmy Wells' possible motives for wanting to deceive Bob, using details from the passage to support their views.

page 153

1. the action or condition of
2. level of existence
3. tending to

page 154

1. She becomes self-conscious about her looks.
2. **Exemplars:** they didn't cook supper; they didn't make up the bed; they neglected all the household tasks

page 155

1. King Midas gives up his greedy wish for riches for the simple life.

2. The story explains the actions of a god, Dionysus.
3. Students should write a short essay explaining why Midas asks for the wish, using details from the passage to support their views.

page 156

1. lowering the body stance
2. people searching for mineral deposits
3. desperate

page 157

1. Thomas Jefferson supports fighting the British to gain independence.
2. **Exemplars:** Similar: both were delegates to the Continental Congress; Different: John Adams did not want independence, while Edward Rutledge wanted independence from Britain

page 158

1. The narrator tried to give herself a perm.
2. upset; **Exemplars:** her mother laments that it looks like the narrator has an afro; the mother thinks her daughter has done it on purpose

page 159

1. almost identical looking
2. angry
3. straw that broke the camel's back
4. unexpected winner

ISTEP+ ANSWER KEY Grade 8

page 3

2. movable

3. center

page 5

2. **Exemplars:** agriculture, the science of cultivating the land; manufacture, to make things by hand or machinery

3. **Exemplars:** farmers live in an agrarian society; manual labor is work done by hand

page 7

2. a bear

3. He can be gruff and grouchy.

page 9

2. **Exemplars:** Title: This passage is about technology in the home, such as television. Graphic and caption: A majority of children are watching television during mealtime. Heading: The author believes that children watch too much television and is suggesting how parents can cut it down.

3. **Exemplars:** The heading "How parents are changing kids' habits."

page 11

2. Lincoln created a document that freed the slaves.

3. Through the North, opponents of slavery hailed Lincoln's actions.

page 13

2. The only things Americans do more than watch television are work and sleep.

3. If you fit the statistical averages, by the age of 20 you will have been exposed to at least 20,000 hours of television.

page 15

2. near the Manor House

3. he does not want the landlord to be suspicious of their actions.

page 17

2. nonfiction

3. facts, dates, and statistics.

page 19

2. third person

3. The pronouns *he* and *she* are used to describe the characters.

page 21

2. Make a Difference Day is a worthy project that everyone should support.

3. He promotes it tirelessly.

page 23

2. **Exemplars:** suggests that early pioneers were a restless breed always looking further West; only the strongest and the bravest made it West; there is no logical explanation for the pioneer's wandering spirit

3. **Exemplars:** The West was settled by a spirited, courageous, and restless breed of men and women.

page 25

2. strong-willed but forgiving

3. She invites him to join her for dinner.

pages 26–35

1. spring

2. **Exemplars:** Modern Celebration: spring prom, Example: Young people dance together, looking to find true love.

3. **Exemplars:** Flowers were put in doors and windows. People made bouquets for one another.

4. cut tree that people dance around.

5. **Exemplars:** Similar: gently dancing around a maypole; Different: moving wildly across the dance floor

6. inform readers

7. Students should choose a favorite holiday and write an essay persuading readers that it is the best holiday.

pages 37–39

1. Bath has a rich history as the site of Britain's only hot springs

2. illnesses

3. **Exemplars:** popular spa: Bath was a well-known Roman-built health resort in ancient times; it became a popular resort again in the eighteenth century when the Roman baths were rediscovered; social and cultural center: Fashionable people of society flocked to Bath to try the baths and socialize in the eighteenth and nineteenth centuries; many fine buildings were constructed during this period that are today considered classic.

4. The author wants to explain the history of Bath.

5. **Exemplars:** as ordinary person: lived in Bath for a time; as author: wrote two novels that were partly set in Bath.

6. **Exemplars:** 54 A.D.: Baths built by Romans; 1755: Baths are rediscovered.

7. to seek out or enjoy the company of others

8. Romans built the first baths at the hot springs in Bath, and the city flourished as a spa in the eighteenth century.

9. Students should write a persuasive essay, using details from the passage to support their views.

pages 40–42

1. Hokusai's habit of trying new styles of art

2. newness and individuality

3. personification

4. **Exemplars:** a restless, unpredictable man: Hokusai lived in as many as a hundred different houses; he changed his name at least thirty times; a great and bold artist: Hokusai was always trying new styles of art; the woodcut print series Thirty-nine Views of Fuji was perhaps his greatest work.

5. breaking free

6. **Exemplars:** Using different objects to paint with: his fingers, toothpicks, an eggshell; Using unusual surfaces to paint on: a grain of rice, a temple door, a courtyard floor.

7. adventurous

8. It gives Hokusai's point of view.

9. Students should write a persuasive letter to a museum and include versions of two exemplars. **Exemplars:** Of all the great artists of Japan, the one Westerners probably like and understand best is Katsushika Hokusai. Hokusai never stayed long with a period or style, but was always off and running to something new. A great show-off, he painted with his fingers, toothpicks, a bottle, an eggshell. *Thirty-six Views of Fuji*, a remarkable set of woodcut prints that tell the story of the countryside around Edo.

pages 43–45

1. dawn

2. a simile

3. John Henry tosses his hammer aside.

4. **Exemplars:** determined: "Bring me two hammers! I'm only getting warmed up"; John Henry gritted his teeth tightly and tried not to hear the roar in his ears or the racing thunder of his heart. confident: "I feel pride hamming at my heart, and I can hardly wait to get started against that machine."; "I'm a steel-driving man and I'm bound to win, because a machine ain't nothing but a machine."

5. **Exemplars:** How does John Henry look?: "as still as the mountain rock," "his shoulders shining like hard coal in the rising sun"; How does John Henry behave?: "[John Henry] sucked in the mountain air," "John Henry swung his hammer, and it rang against the drill"

6. is telling the story in the dialect of the region where it is set

7. nighttime was approaching

8. the judges announce John Henry has won the contest

9. Students should write an essay that explores the theme and and include versions of two exemplars. **Exemplars:** "...I feel pride hammering at my heart, and I can hardly wait to get started against that machine," [John Henry] sucked in the mountain air. "I feel powerful free, Li'l Willie."; John Henry ground his teeth together and tried not to hear the roar in his ears or the racing thunder of his heart. "I'll go until I drop," he gasped. "I'm a steel-driving man and I'm bound to win, because a machine ain't nothing but a machine."

pages 47–61

1. in the first person

2. **Exemplars:** She noticed many signs that her sister loved the jacket and wanted it. Her sister's enthusiasm for helping find the jacket seemed out of character. Her sister wanted a suitcase that locked. This wasn't the first time that she suspected her sister of taking missing clothing.

3. simile

4. **Exemplars:** What Lizzie thought her sister was like: a liar, jealous, sneaky, guilty; What her sister was really like: caring, honest, innocent, helpful, generous

5. Lizzie apologizes to her sister for ever suspecting her.

6. animal skins.

7. more comfortable

8. shoemaker

9. **Exemplars:** American Society: shoe crazy; Example: We have shoes for every type of activity. Shoe fashion is big business today.

10. The look of shoes has always been as important as their practicality.

11. Students should write a persuasive essay about a favorite article of clothing and provide support for their ideas.

pages 63–82

1. loving

2. **Exemplars:** Attitude: He does not like the moonlight. Example: I gaz'd a while/On her cold smile/Too cold—too cold for me.

3. **Exemplars:** Proud Evening Star,/In thy glory afar; For joy to my heart/Is the proud part/Thou bearest in Heav'n at night; And more I admire/Thy distant fire

4. to help with the rhythm of the poem

5. midnight

6. prefers the starlight over the moonlight

7. mutual

8. They could not grow and spread.

9. **Exemplars:** It takes the bark of three Pacific yew trees to produce enough pure taxol for one cancer patient's treatment. If the bark is removed from a yew tree, the tree cannot survive. Pacific yews cannot be grown from seeds.

10. Taxol will continue to be used to treat cancer.

11. **Exemplars:** 1) an encyclopedia, a reference book, a science text; 2) These words are the scientific name for the tree and are in Latin and are set apart for this reason.

12. inform readers

13. Students should write a persuasive essay, using details from the passage to support their views.

pages 83–102

1. The wonders of nature are all around us.

2. **Exemplars:** Reason: She is fascinated because the bird is so alive and interesting to watch. Example: "He bit an Angleworm in halves/And ate the fellow, raw"; "And then he drank a Dew/From a convenient Grass—"; "And then hopped sidewise to the Wall/To let a Beetle pass—"; "He glanced with rapid eyes/That hurried all around—"

3. **Exemplars:** 1) she compares his eyes to beads; 2) a simile

4. thoughtful

5. the ocean

6. sight

7. biography

8. learned to read

9. **Exemplars:** He faced possible capture by his former master if he stayed in the United States. He had given details about his former life in his autobiography, making him a target for recapture.

10. was exposed and went to prison

11. **Exemplars:** The sentence is in quotation marks because it is a direct quote from someone who had heard Douglass speak; He is saying that they were moved and persuaded by his arguments against slavery.

12. civil rights leader

13. Students should write a persuasive essay about an admired American and provide support for their own views.

pages 103–122

1. thoughtful

2. the process of making decisions

3. **Exemplars:** "Then took the others, just as fair,/And having perhaps the better claim"; "I took the one less traveled by,/And that has made all the difference."

4. **Exemplars:** Reason: He took it thinking it would be more of an adventure than the more-traveled road. Example: "Because it was grassy and wanted wear"; "I took the one less traveled by"

5. Where no evidence of travel was visible

6. taking the less traveled road made a difference in his life

7. It presents a scientific explanation.

8. study a cyclical process of nature

9. **Exemplars:** People are thrilled and pleased by the brilliant colors. They can find comfort and understanding of death's role in their own lives.

10. They are concealed.

11. **Exemplars:** 1) It is a metaphor. 2) The barbed wire has pointy knots of wire throughout its length. When the frost turns these knots white, they look like a string of stars.

12. inclined to like something in advance

13. Students should write a persuasive essay and provide support for their own views.

page 124

1. devise a plan for killing the old man

2. I made up my mind to take the life of the old man, and thus rid myself of the eye forever

3. **Exemplars:** The narrator will confess his crime to the police. The narrator will fight his guilt and not confess to the police.

page 125

1. She wants an umbrella, but is not sure that she should take Eugenie's.

2. **Exemplars:** The narrator wants to open it. The narrator wants to twirl it around by its handle. The narrator wants to carry the umbrella the way other girls do.

3. Students' essays should offer an appropriate resolution to the narrator's conflict.

page 126

1. restless

2. not

3. to make better

4. together

page 127

1. to add suspense and tension

2. **Exemplars:** "I could, however, see that his face was deadly pale and filled with horror and loathing"; "There broke from the silence of the night the most horrible cry to which I have ever listened"; "a hoarse yell of pain and fear and anger all mingled in the one dreadful shriek"; "It struck cold to our hearts"

page 128

1. humorous

2. the setting of the story

3. **Exemplars:** "and mind, whatever a blue jay feels, he can put into language"; "why, you never see a blue jay get stuck for a word"; "And another thing: I've noted a good deal..."

4. Students' essays should explain whether they think the speaker in the passage believes that blue jays can really talk.

page 129

1. in an eager manner

2. full of

3. at the same time

4. verb to a noun

page 130

1. uncomfortable

2. got passengers from one place to another

3. **Exemplars:** Similar: both designed for comfort, both designed for overnight travel; Difference: Palace Car had chandeliers; Palace Car had gourmet food

page 131

1. a riverbank

2. summer

3. **Exemplars:** Alice doesn't like reading a book if it doesn't have any pictures in it;

Alice wonders whether the pleasure is making a daisy-chain is worth the trouble of getting up to pick the daisies

4. Students should tell whether they agree with Alice and provide support for their own views.

page 132

1. words that come after

2. not reasonable

3. the study of the mind

4. trilogy

page 133

1. it meant that the United States had continued to expand

2. **Exemplars:** patriotic: "there is not in America a more loyal man than I"; "There cannot be a man who loves the old flag as I do." desperate: "O Captain, I know I am dying. I cannot get home"; "But tell me— tell me something—tell me everything, Danforth, before I die!"

page 134

1. first person

2. **Exemplars:** self exile: "I awoke to the bitter knowledge that in order just to continue to love the land of my birth, I was expected to leave it"; "…to stay willingly in a beloved but brutal place is to risk losing the love"; dispossession: "My father inherited nothing of material value from his father"; "in order just to continue to love the land of my birth, I was expected to leave it."

3. Students should explain how the author feels about her native country, using details from the passage to support their own views.

page 135

1. You show how they are different.

2. shows one way two different things are alike.

3. disagree about something

4. happen at the same time

page 136

1. Humans migrate for many different reasons.

2. why people move from one place to another

3. **Exemplars:** Some people migrate because conditions in their home countries "push" them to leave. People may be poor, unable to find work, or buy land. Other people move because they want to live better lives.

page 137

1. It tells a story and has a character.

2. **Exemplars:** Words: "So I drafted a petition for the resident to sign to try to stop the developer from building." Actions: Sometimes he sat quietly for hours, studying animal behavior.

3. Students should predict what Andy will do next, using details from the passage to support their predictions.

page 138

1. barely

2. evened out

3. corridors and passageways

page 139

1. The fire burned more vividly than the sun.

2. The narrator's house burned down.

3. fact, opinion

page 140

1. support a woman's right to vote

2. rhetorical question: "Are women persons?"

3. Students should evaluate the persuasiveness of Anthony's argument, using details from the passage to support their ideas.

page 141

1. safety

2. neglect

3. meekly

page 142

1. got

2. forceful

3. **Exemplars:** broke: escaped, "of their own will"; bursting: overflowing, "with love"

page 143

1. personification

2. **Exemplars:** repetition: "Blow from the mountains, blow from the west…Blow, blow!"; alliteration: "wind of the west, we wait for you"

3. Students should describe how the speaker feels about being outdoors, using details from the poem to support their ideas.

page 144

1. full of

2. adverb

3. noun to an adjective

4. is full of courage

page 145

1. Elizabeth's career choices are very limited as a woman.

2. **Exemplars:** I don't sew well, though I could teach music. But I want to be a doctor.

page 146

1. lyric

2. **Exemplars:** sunset: death, fading of glory; dark hills: mortality, no one lives forever

3. Students should identify the poet's perspective on war, using details from the poem to support their ideas.

page 147

1. ending
2. decisive
3. to shut

page 148

1. his hoofs were worn down to the hair
2. **Exemplars:** Maria is extremely fond of Sancho. She hugs him and cries when she saw him. She feeds him hot tamales nearly every day. She was nervous over the prospect of losing her pet.

page 149

1. movement of the characters
2. **Exemplars:** Although Julia is trying to hide it, something is deeply troubling her. Julia can't control her emotions any longer and her mistress doesn't understand why she is acting like this.
3. Students should describe the events that led to this scene, using details from the poem to support their views.

page 150

1. watches the game
2. examines it closely
3. see better
4. dramatic in an eye-catching way

page 151

1. people call asking for another Shlemiel
2. he cannot find his way home
3. **Exemplars:** looks in a telephone book in the drugstore

page 152

1. what a woman's role should be
2. **Exemplars:** Character Trait: ambitious; Supporting Dialogue: "I'm going to be remarkable! Character Trait: outspoken; Supporting Dialogue: "Why aren't you nice and quiet like your sister Margot?"

3. Students should explore why Anne wants to go to Paris, using details from the poem to support their ideas.

page 153

1. helps get things done
2. follows the original
3. do them step by step
4. to make by hand

page 154

1. Valentine is back to his old criminal ways.
2. Valentine Strikes Again
3. **Exemplars:** A week after the release of Valentine…there was a…safe-burglary done in Richmond, Indiana, with no clue to the author. By comparing notes, a remarkable similarity in the methods of the burglaries was noticed. "That's Dandy Jim Valentine's autograph. He's resumed business…."

page 155

1. the flower Narcissus and an echo came to be
2. **Exemplars:** Love for the Greeks could be a destructive force; The Greeks placed a high value on physical beauty.

page 156

1. comes into a country
2. surprise
3. moved to another state

page 157

1. Susan B. Anthony and woman's suffrage
2. **Exemplars:** What did Susan do after getting out of jail? Were Susan's friend in Washington able to help her advance her cause?

page 158

1. the reform movements of his day

2. **Exemplars:** Ring out: struggle between the social classes; unjust laws; all the wars of the past; Ring in: equality for all people; love of truth and right; a thousand years of peace

3. Students should evaluate the poet's hope for the future, using details from the poem to support their ideas.

page 159

1. barbecue

2. raccoon

3. bayou

4. shoe